GW00701528

This book was donated
in memory
Of
Jane O'Hear 1956-2018

30127 08647923 0

Dedication

To my ever-supportive husband Trevor
and all my friends.

Lisa Primrose

You Just Hear That Word Cancer and You Just Can't Take It

AUSTIN MACAULEY™
PUBLISHERS LTD.

A CIP catalogue record for this title is available from the British Library.

ISBN 9781786298201 (Paperback)
ISBN 9781786298218 (Hardback)
ISBN 9781786298225 (E-Book)
www.austinmacauley.com

First Published (2017)
Austin Macauley Publishers Ltd.™
25 Canada Square
Canary Wharf
London
E14 5LQ

Acknowledgments

The Freeman Hospital, Newcastle Upon Tyne
The University Hospital of North Durham
Miss S E Green, Consultant
Mr Reubin, Consultant

OCTOBER 2012

2ND OCT TUESDAY 9.45 AM

You just hear that word cancer.

The day was Tuesday the date was the 2nd of October 2012 and the time was 9.45am. This is a day I will never forget it will stay with me forever.

I had been experiencing blood while passing stools for a couple of months so I decided to bite the bullet and make an appointment (Initially with Dr. Harbinson). He examined me and seemed concerned

I was made another appointment for the second of October at 9.45am. I had a colonoscopy. I was so nervous I asked for a general anaesthetic. This was agreed and so the procedure was done successfully. However, the result was not the result I had been expecting. Miss Green who carried out the test confirmed what I had been dreading. I had cancer, rectal carcinoma to be precise. I had so many unwanted emotions racing around inside me and the burning question Why why me? I was (and still am) in a total state of incomprehensible shock and untold grief.

Here I am I am 46 and I don't eat unhealthily, don't drink, don't smoke, so how has this happened to me?

I made two decisions there and then.

1. Not to tell my family I mean they would just add to my stress.
2. I would beat this unwelcome intrusion. It is not wanted now or ever.

So on the 5th October Trevor and I got remarried. After what had been diagnosed I felt it was the right time. And after Julie had lost David to cancer I feel I had learned to appreciate what I had.

The following days all just seemed to blur into one. I have up and down days, then I just think of when I will be rid of this enemy. I picked this journal design (birds) cos soon I know I'll be as free (from the rectal carcinoma) as a bird to get back on to my life again. I cry every now and again and I know I have a long hard battle ahead but I survived neonatal meningitis so I will survive this nightmare.

I find that writing this all down, I can vent my feelings of being scared. I am bound to be scared as I haven't had cancer before. I can be immensely proud of myself for going to the doctor early enough therefore giving myself a 100% chance of beating this; what I will call inconvenience.

I have decided not to tell my family because of what my mother said to me one Christmas (2005) she said to me, You weren't supposed to be here.

I said, But you invited me.

She said, You were supposed to be dead at birth.

This hit me like a collapsing house and she had been drinking and was therefore drunk! I said to her, Oh that's it!! That's the finish! and have never made contact with her ever since. Who in their right mind would, after someone saying that to you? I even moved house twice without telling her. Nothing healthwise has gone right for me since she said this. The family is so negative minded and I am determined to beat this not for them but for Trevor and myself and Lorraine and Kenneth.

11TH OCT THURSDAY

Another day with my rectal carcinoma. I hate the way it makes me feel so tired and sometimes weepy. I also can't seem to settle in one position cos I have sciatica also. This is hurting too! I went to the UHND for my very first CT scan this was done by a professional CT scanner. The person who did it was also very professional his name was Jonathan Slater and he put me at ease in no time at all. I was very nervous here again something new was happening to me <u>yet again</u>. I had to drink a litre of water as usual for these tests! My poor bladder couldn't wait to get out of there and back to Trevor who has been supportive.

We then went to McDonalds at Arnison and Sally told us she was 4 months pregnant after 17 years and IVF etc! Bless her.

I told Kendra etc I had cancer. This was hard as I used to work with her. I still have ups and downs but I am just very thankful I plucked up the courage to go and get checked, however undignified the process. This is step 2 complete and one step closer to eliminating this thing!

12TH OCT FRIDAY

Another day with my rectal carcinoma. I text Jeanette my friend at Team Valley yesterday and she texts back saying that she can't stop thinking of me and that I have to stay positive. I try and do this every day and I know I will get through it. When I get up on a morning I feel totally different now. I know I have a hell of a year ahead but I will pull through to the positive side of recovery. I seem to get tired round about 2.00pm and know I need to rest. It is the hardest test which I will pass. I'm not going anywhere yet.

13TH OCT SATURDAY

I seem to have had rather a low day today, up and down. The postman brought me a nice surprise though which cheered me up. A House of Commons notelet and a message from Kevan Jones our MP, bless him! We went to McDonalds and Jeanette hugged me. She said she was thinking about me all night bless her too. I guess I am just plain scared what was ahead of me. I <u>will</u> get through this I am strong determined person who has come through neonatal meningitis so this is no different. I have enlisted help from a guardian angel who I pray to on an evening whilst praying she (or he) will help me I know.

14TH OCT SUNDAY

I awoke today and began to feel nauseous, but I know I must eat to keep my strength up. I just feel so sickly I hope it goes away. We went to see Jeanette and had a coffee and a chat. Then we went to the coast where the rollers (waves) were mega, man. We had a cup of tea and I just sat and watched the waves thinking Why why me! Positivity is the name of the game. No one is going to do this for me.

15TH OCT MONDAY

I woke up feeling down and sickly, probably nerves. I will get through this awful traumatic event in my life but still can't come to terms with the fact it chose me. We went to McDonalds and saw Jeanette's daughter, Hayley What a lovely girl she is, like mother like daughter, I always say. We had a coffee and a chat and met baby Isaac who I kept calling Jacob because we were discussing biblical baby names making a comeback. I always feel better after a good chat takes my mind off my rectal carcinoma and all the mental anguish it brings. But I am a strong lady.

16TH OCT TUESDAY

It was pension day today and we went to Krispy Kreme Doughnuts for a change. I had a white chocolate pistachio doughnut which was well tasty and a hazelnut latte. We normally go to Costa but this was different. We then went to McDonalds and saw Jeanette and Steve just went through drive through seeing Steve at 3.30pm tomorrow. I was a little bit more positive today. Can only build on it.

17TH OCT WEDNESDAY

Today I woke after another night of being unable to get to sleep straight away. I am so proud of myself for going to get it checked. If I hadn't then, who knows? I have the worst bit to come but the results will be good ones because the radiotherapy will kill it off gradually and then I will have an operation to remove it. Then I will be free of cancer.

Trevor is being so supportive of me and it is reassuring to know he is there. I now listen to Radio 3 and heard the Second Movement of Dvorak's Cello Concerto (Panthers Piece). I immediately felt at ease as I was back home listening to it while looking at my dead cat Panthers grave. I miss her and I am sure Panther wants me well again as do I. Steve was unavailable.

18TH OCT THURSDAY

I awoke this morning to a lovely sunny day so this helps a bit, but I am doing really well I think for a 46-year-old who has been diagnosed with colorectal (rectal) carcinoma. We went on the usual coffee runs. Tom and Ida were at Arnison at 11 am. They get on my nerves. We had 2 coffees there and on the way there we saw a poor rabbit who I named Bristles cos of her colour. She was wet and cold and just sitting in the middle of the road at Waldridge Fell shed sadly died by the time we had come back to check on her. I have had a positive day (apart from Bristles).

19TH OCT FRIDAY

I had some good news today which made me smile. The hospital rang and I have an appointment on Monday at 10 am with Miss Green at the UHND. So something will finally get started. So it's see ya rectal carcinoma: wouldn't wanna be ya!

20TH OCT SATURDAY

I had my MRI scan today and I had some silent tears. I call them this cos they just fall without warning! I am scared about what is going to happen on Monday at 10am at UHND, what will the results say? I know that they will cure me but it is so hard man! I will beat this cancer. She played some Coldplay and I fell asleep in the machine! Trust me, eh? Trevor had a football coupon off (29.32).

21ST OCT SUNDAY

I had a relaxing day and I finished my mosaic cat pictures. I have 2 left to do. Listened to Coldplay X + Y of course. Coffee was slotted in! We went to Starbucks and I tried a spicy pumpkin loaf and had a grande latte I should have had hazelnut in but there was none least of my worries! Sore bumhole, unable to sit!

22ND OCT MONDAY

D-Day! Today I had my 10am appointment with Miss Green. She is marvellous. Tomorrow I go in to the DSU for a nodule in my left groin to be removed and analysed. I am then waiting for a PET scan to determine to what the thing is that showed up on the CT scan. I literally feel like I am at breaking point, that is why I am writing it all down in order to rid this breaking point. I am strong so it'll be OK.

23RD OCT TUESDAY

Well today is the day the ball gets rolling. Up at 6am to have toast and coffee then I had a wash and made myself presentable. Bursting with both nerves and pride for getting it caught early. I went in and was weighed, I now weigh 11 stone 4lb. I was then checked in to the DSU. In the waiting room waiting to go to theatre not long now. Dancing Queen plays on Smooth FM. Look at clock, it was 1.30pm the next thing I knew I was down at theatre now. 1.50pm the very last thing I remember is looking at the clock outside theatre.

It now said 1.55pm. Came round on the ward at 3pm no Trevor, still in reception. Had coffee and toast after sleep. Dr Sripathy was on rounds, saw me and was sad to learn I had cancer. I asked him to tell Trevor I was awake and eating toast and coffee. I then got dressed with Trevor's help and we left. PET scan on Friday at 1.30pm at the Freeman.

24TH OCT WEDNESDAY

The day after. I am still chocker with anaesthesia so I have to take it easy really drowsy do nothing but sleep, apart from going off for coffee of course!

25TH OCT THURSDAY

Ruby's memorial, bless her. Had the flu jab today. Still drowsy. Went for coffee. Beginning to feel more confident now. Had my first bath so I washed my hair ready for my PET scan tomorrow. God I hope the anomalies aren't abnormal but benign!

26TH OCT FRIDAY

This day I have dreaded has arrived but I <u>know</u> that everything is now moving swiftly. I arrived at the Freeman and we managed to find a parking space in Car Park One (I know!) The staff there were above and beyond the call of duty. Nothing was too much trouble. Mr Jenkinson was really first class he explained things as he was going along.

As did Catherine. They even tuned in Radio 3 for me. I was injected with a radioactive sugar solution then rested in a nice warm room and fell asleep! Then I was moved to the scanner with Mr Jenkinson's and Trevor's help, where I found Radio 3 again and fell asleep again.

I came round and was explained as to what was going to happen next. I will get all the results on 06.11.2012.

Each day that comes and goes I am feeling more and more positive that I am going to beat this unwelcome visitor.

27TH OCT SATURDAY

I awoke as usual extremely early (3.45am) so I make a fruit tea and an ordinary tea for Trevor. He has been amazing, he really has. My frontal area is throbbing and I am unable to sit for long periods. This is due to the rectal area. I have to lie on my side. Trevor and I drink our tea while I open up to him. I seem to have accepted the fact I have cancer but I think that's why I am so disturbed in sleep. We look for something to watch (Bid TV). I am on Diazepam so I take one and the fruit tea does its trick and I fall asleep. Temporarily away from my cancer I dream and know I'm cured.

28TH OCT SUNDAY

I awake again and there is the word again Cancer. What a strange day. I had the bears in my bag and had them out at McDonalds then they've just vanished. I am not supposed to get upset because of my condition but I am so so sad. I just don't know where they are I hope to God they turn up.

29TH OCT MONDAY

Good news day! Miss S E Green rang with news that my biopsy results had come back and it was <u>good</u> news! The lymph nodes in my lung and groin were just reactive lymph nodes. Trevor and I were over the moon to say the least!

30TH OCT TUESDAY

We saw Steve for coffee and talked. It is increasingly more uncomfortable to sit for long periods. I have resorted to a cushion in the car but all that does is transfers the pain. It is undignified as I do a lot of farting which can't be helped!

31ST OCT WEDNESDAY

A day at Hexham. Bought a better cushion at Poundstretcher. Gave brown cushion to cat. She has slept on it <u>all</u> day! Perfect visits today still hurts though. Sciatica has been OK today also.

NOVEMBER 2012

1ST NOV THURSDAY

Went for coffee. I bought them. I still get very tired very quickly sadly.

2ND NOV FRIDAY

Good news day!

Exactly 4 weeks ago since I was diagnosed with a rectal carcinoma (which was the <u>worst</u> day in my life). Today it was my friend's husband's funeral. But I had also had a phone call from Miss Green which Trevor took as I was asleep after a rough night <u>trying</u> to sleep. The PET scan I had at the Freeman Centre came back as clear, the cancer hasn't spread. I was so happy when I awoke and was told the news. I got dressed and went and told all my friends at the various McDonalds. They were all so pleased for me as was Trevor. I just can't wait to get the treatment started and zap this unwanted intrusion in my life.

3RD NOV SATURDAY

Up at 11am. We went for coffees as we always do. Then we came home and watched Manchester United v Arsenal. Man United won. I put my coupon on. We went to see Skyfall at the Metrocentre and I spent the evening trying to get comfortable while sitting watching but because of my rectal carcinoma it is becoming increasingly more difficult. I had a coffee from Costa to take in. Skyfall was excellent. Counting down to the 6th November when I get the next steps.

4TH NOV SUNDAY

I have been extremely tired today but went out for coffee and came home and helped prepare dinner. Watched footie. Slept again all afternoon!

5TH NOV MONDAY

My backside is quite sore after going to the toilet. Distressed because it is uncomfortable to sit a long time seeing Miss Green at 10.15am tomorrow. Good!

6TH NOV TUESDAY

I went to UHND and saw not Miss Green but Dr Bain. He said I had to try and lose at least one stone in weight. Miss Green had a family bereavement, bless her. I do hope she's OK. I gave a thank you card for her as she is literally saving my life. The cancer hasn't spread to the groin area and lung. This is uplifting and excellent news so off to McDs we went to celebrate. I topped my phone up today. When I was weighed I was 11st 11 lbs with all clothes and jacket and shoes on. President Obama was the winner in the 2012 US elections. Sore bottom today, can't sit not for much longer now.

7TH NOV WEDNESDAY

Went to see Dennis whose wife has breast cancer. Clive Dunne dies aged 92. Sore again both ends. Ouch! Can't sit. I am though remaining extremely positive because I am surrounded by good people with good intentions, love and support.

8TH NOV THURSDAY

My friend Julie Hedley would have been 48 today. I awoke today in pain as usual but I am determined to stay upbeat! We went for coffee and chatted to Dennis whose wife Chris has cancer of the breast. We then went down the Death Road and had another. We came home about 2.30pm and I was tired so I slept. I did a bit of mosaic cat and went to sleep on the settee about 7.30pm. I get so tired so quick. We watched Ice Road Truckers (holy fuck).

9TH NOV FRIDAY

Had coffee at Team Valley and Arnison. Talked to Jeanette about yesterday's accident she had. She had an awful bruise on her wrist and had jarred her shoulder. Bloody charvers! Bit sore again, today still unable to sit! I can't wait for my treatment to begin but won't be going to the ATP tour now till this time next year. The O2 rang and were really nice. Haven't heard from chemo yet I will though. Come on!

10TH NOV SATURDAY

I am in so much pain today with the area concerned. I am unable to sit again and go to the toilet successfully. So I am on the painkillers. I put my football coupon on as usual because it is important to do the same routine. I am just so bloody sore I am sure tomorrow will be a better day.

11TH NOV SUNDAY

Remembrance Sunday. I am still sore today. I should hear from the Freeman this week though about commencement of treatment. I am remaining positive and upbeat however. Went for coffee today.

12TH NOV MONDAY

I have been so tired and so sore again my perineum is really uncomfortable. I have to shift myself around to get comfy I find lying on my side eases it for a while. Still no word from the Freeman sometime this week I would think.

13TH NOV TUESDAY

DOCTORS AT 9AM

Up at 7.30am in excruciating pain with sciatica and the rectal carcinoma practically hobbled in to Dr Rochester and sat gingerly down as well as squirming to get comfy hasn't eased at all. Left a message for Karen/Fiona.

14TH NOV WEDNESDAY

Drew a tenner out and treated us to a Starbucks. I am still in a great deal of pain and still can't sit. Heard from Karen and have an appointment with the Freeman on the 20th November. Great stuff get the ball rolling now.

15TH NOV THURSDAY

Still in a great deal of pain. Walking like John Wayne. The quicker I get seen to, the better. Grandpas birthday but too ill to take flowers to Hebburn Cemetery. Remaining positive.

16TH NOV FRIDAY

Pension day, so we went to Costa. Gingerbread latte was tasty man. I will do this in the future when I am cured. Bad night last night so not much sleep couldn't get comfy in bed. On and off the loo with numerous craps all different shades and smells! Felt as sick as a dog all afternoon. Can't wait for Tuesday to get the ball rolling

17TH NOV SATURDAY

We went for coffee and I was unable to sit. Put my football coupon on as usual. Still in much discomfort but not as many craps today. I <u>will</u> beat cancer.

18TH NOV SUNDAY

We went to McDonalds again to see my friends. Durham is shut for 3 weeks. Still can't sit very long as it knacks in between the legs, man. I must however remain positive that it will be cured. I will be like a piece of back bacon this time next year CURED! Coupons never came off again bloody Chelsea, Man United (against Norwich!)

19TH NOV MONDAY

Man came about Lassie at 36 Lime St with his noise recorder. What a windbag, Trevor said when he left us. She didn't bark a lot! Henry has vanished. In agony sitting, using brown settee to lie flat on which helps. Hosp app tomorrow. This is the start factor right here. Bring it on!

20TH NOV TUESDAY

Jacks birthday. Today's the day! I awoke at 7am and got ready. We got there at around 9. The oncologist was really nice. He went through everything in minute and perfectly clear detail. I will start radiotherapy in 1-2 weeks there will then be a break of 10 weeks approx. followed an operation. I will then have to wear a colostomy bag. So I will then call myself a colostomy bag! Just for fun of course it's my way of coping with it What a day! I couldn't sit in the car or in the hospital. This was explained to me as to why. Ouch en masse!

21ST NOV WEDNESDAY

Woke up feeling like shit! I feel as if I am carrying a house brick in my back passage and I am finding it incredibly more and more difficult to sit down anywhere. It knacks!

22ND NOV THURSDAY

Bloody spasms in my back end knack again! Can't sit and have a good cry today. Chin up.

23RD NOV FRIDAY

Put coupons on for tomorrow. McDonalds today. Can't sit again. Had a visit and it was OK. I really feel humiliated asking Trevor to clean my arse but it must be worse for him. Just want it out!

24TH NOV SATURDAY

Costa today as carers allowance. Extremely sore today can't walk around. 4 out of 4 on coupon so far.

25TH NOV SUNDAY

Extremely uncomfortable again today. A few accidents. Coupons come off! Yay!

26TH NOV MONDAY

Can't seem to sit again for long. Cushion between legs seem to help. Delicious soup for tea. I am so tired today.

27TH NOV TUESDAY

No phone call yet. Gary Speeds first memorial. Friends birthday (60) drop card off. Still sore but learning to cope. Mammoth shit. Rest again today.

28TH NOV WEDNESDAY

In pain again can't sit down or lie in comfort. I can't wait to start treatment and get rid of this tumour.

29TH NOV THURSDAY

Appointment today at 11am. Get sheet of treatment schedule, will begin 7th December. Get in!

30TH NOV FRIDAY

Still in extreme pain in between legs. Alison(MacMillan) rang. Trevor spoke to her first then put me on. I told her about the feeling between my legs and she said I was doing all the right things and the feeling will ease after the radiotherapy. God I can't wait.

DECEMBER 2012

1ST DEC SATURDAY

Niece Heidi marries. Have a car prang. This affects me and Trevor. I could hardly walk again. I had to go in the bath to ensure stiffness didn't set in! I have been so tired again today. Can't wait to start radiotherapy and chemotherapy next week! Bring it on I say!

2ND DEC SUNDAY

No luck with coupon. Have a stiff and painful left leg. May be off yesterday. Didn't go out I was too nervous again. Had a few visits to the toilet and it was OK just the amount of times. Still very sore can't sit for long periods. Can't wait for Friday.

3RD DEC MONDAY

We went for coffee in the hire car to Team Valley. Had a coffee and while there, had an accident so I had to get a wash. I find this so embarrassing but it can't be helped. We came home and tidied my room up. I watched Neighbours then had a cat nap. Went to the doctors at 11am to see Dr Thorp. I have a torn ligament in my left thigh after Saturday and poor Trevor has whiplash. Nasty.

4TH DEC TUESDAY

Molly (car) came to be taken to Doncaster to try and be repaired. I cried because I knew her significance. We picked her up on the 2nd October 2012 the day I had been diagnosed with my colorectal malignant tumour. I went to Craghead PO and drew out 20. Still sore. Told McD at Consett about it. They were very sympathetic and supportive.

5TH DEC WEDNESDAY

What a truly horrible day this was. It is blood freezing which won't help me. But the treatment is drawing ever nearer. But even when I am cured and I <u>will be</u>, I will be left with the scar of being given this painful thing. I can't sit unless I am on a cushion and am on Diazepam for distress but it is helping.

6TH DEC THURSDAY

Terrible pain today. Can't sit down for long. Dying to do my mosaic owl. Can only do 1 or 2 squares at most then I have to put it away. At hospital tomorrow to start treatment to eventually zap this bloody thing!

7TH DEC FRIDAY

At Freeman got tablets to take. 6 of each bloody hell man!

8TH DEC SATURDAY

Quite a painful day today. Arnison centre McD reopens, had coffee, and talked to Dennis and Keiron. Put coupon on and looks like it is heading for the bin

9TH DEC SUNDAY

Didn't venture too far today. Went to McDonalds Arnison. Back for footie. Just lay and slept on and off. Tomorrow is a very big day for me. This unwelcome visitor gets zapped it's the beginning of the end of you brother. Get lost.

DECEMBER - TREATMENT COMMENCES

10TH DEC MONDAY

Chemotherapy and radiotherapy begin at the Freeman. I lay on my tummy and did nothing but fart. I requested Coldplay while this was going on. When it finished I was sore and walked like John Wayne again. I came home and slept (lovely man!) Back again tomorrow.

11TH DEC TUESDAY

More radiotherapy this is quite relaxing in a way because I know it is being zapped to buggery little by little day by day. I was dehydrated when it was over so drank like a fish. Slept quite well stopped Diazepam.

12TH DEC WEDNESDAY

Sore again! One more day closer to being cured.

13TH DEC THURSDAY

Back again got in pretty quick. More zapping. I fell asleep on the table. Christmas music playing while it was being done. Darkness track kept jumping till the end (dust I reckon) typical!

14TH DEC FRIDAY

Today was the end of my first week. One week down four to go. I can and will do this.

15TH DEC SATURDAY

Oops! It seems like I am not getting any messages of when to go. So I am just going anyway. This is NOT GOOD for my rectum. Sometimes it happens sometimes not. I need to re-educate my brain to send these go Lisa messages.

16TH DEC SUNDAY

I have tried to resist the urge to go done OK till 11pm!

17TH DEC MONDAY

2nd week of treatment. 2 down. 3 to go.

18TH DEC TUESDAY

More radiotherapy treatment. I had a huge crap (sausage) and I just slept again I am just <u>so</u> tired. Amy plays some Coldplay while the treatment is getting done. Zap the. Is what I say. Each zapping it is getting smaller. More again tomorrow.

19TH DEC WEDNESDAY

More radiotherapy. It seems to be shrinking as I can now lie down and sleep. Bloody hell I can sleep for England I am so tired. This is a positive sign that I can lie down and sleep. Nearly the end of my second week yay man.

20TH DEC THURSDAY

I have quite bad toilet visits today at least 5! More radiotherapy. Coldplay is played track 4 Fix You. Scrubs borrowed!

21ST DEC FRIDAY

Taxi booked for Xmas Eve then I am off Boxing Day and New Year's Day. More radiotherapy not bad. Today restless in bed though. End of 2nd week!!!

22ND DEC SATURDAY

No tablets this weekend. I put a coupon on 3 right so far.

23RD DEC SUNDAY

No tablets yay!

24TH DEC MONDAY

I went in for treatment today by a PTS to give Trevor a rest from driving. Got in straight away home by 1pm then we went shopping for Xmas pressies.

25TH DEC TUESDAY

Nothing today.

28TH DEC FRIDAY

Nothing today. Nothing till 31st.

31ˢᵀ DEC MONDAY

It is Mr John Shields first memorial (1 year). I put some
flowers by his door.

GOODBYE 2012
(and good riddance)

HELLO 2013: Be Good To Me
JANUARY

1ST JAN TUESDAY

Day off: NYD

2ND JAN WEDNESDAY

We got there in excellent time! I got in on time and was imaged from a different angle, the slab was hard, man! I just go to sleep. Chelsea knocked me out of a clean sweep!

3RD JAN THURSDAY

Awful day today never seen so much shit on my undies. Radiotherapy done zap a bit more of it away. <u>Should</u> be just about gone!

4TH JAN FRIDAY

Another zapping! Coldplay plays. Instant sleep!

7TH JAN MONDAY

Struggled to get into position but Sally and Michaela seem to understand and so they helped me extremely sore after. Couldn't face cream being put on silly really! Instant sleep lovely!

8TH JAN TUESDAY

Much better today, allowed Trevor to apply cream and gel lovely relief. Sally and Michaela got me into position. Sleeping much better.

9TH JAN WEDNESDAY

Another zapping! It must be nearly gone (if not altogether).

10TH JAN THURSDAY

Here we go again! Another zapping. So tired just sleep. So bloody sore!

11TH JAN FRIDAY

Still sore after another zapping! Still there's only three left after today.

14TH JAN MONDAY

Happy birthday Lorraine! Another zapping, more Coldplay. The staff are extremely helpful. 2 more after today. Went for a hot chocolate.

15TH JAN TUESDAY

Back again! More zappings, more Coldplay. Fell asleep and it only took 5 minutes!

16TH JAN WEDNESDAY

Ee, well here we are again! Room One today, no Coldplay, different room. Just Sally and some bloke today! Expect I'll be back in room 7 tomorrow.

END OF CHEMO AND RADIOTHERAPY

EPILOGUE

One Year on!

WEDNESDAY 2ND OCTOBER 2013

To mark the day Trevor and I booked a table at Sorella Sorella and had a very tasty afternoon meal. I have had scans since and I am very pleased to say I am cleared. We sat in Sorella Sorella and we talked about that date one year ago.